AN ANALYSIS OF ACCLIMATIZATION IN ISHMAEL SCOTT REED'S THE TERRIBLE TWOS AND THE TERRIBLE THREES

DR C SWATHI

ISBN 979-888530773-4

Contents

Foreword

The main focus is on the inspection of the characters based on their behavioural aspects and analyzing the characters based on pliable techniques. The concept of adaptation involves adjustment and getting adjusted to the new conditions. Adapting to the atmosphere supports people to face the challenges andopportunities of the atmosphere in an optimistic way. The characters in the fiction habituate to the surroundings and do things based on the group to which the people belong. Reed through his exploration of new concepts and unique detective techniques, has paved way for most of the readers to learn about various traditions and to develop their adaptive techniques to excel in life.

CHAPTER ONE

An Analysis of Acclimatization in Ishmael Scott Reed's ThTerrible Twos and The Terrible Threes

African American literature has been created in the United States by writers of African descent. African American literature has been written about, by and at times it has been written in particular for African American people. This unique genre started during the eighteenth and nineteenth centuries. The most notable personalities in this genre are the poet Phillis Wheatley and the most popular orator Fredrick Douglass. This literature become popular with the Harlem Renaissance and it continues at present with many popular authors in the United States.

Most of the African American writers wrote about the suppression of Black people which include themes like racism, black identity, struggle and liberty. All those writers continuously strived hard to get liberty for the longing eyes of the black people. The only motto of African American writers was to get freedom which was in a height and which the black people could not reach. Therefore, most of the writers repeated the themes, in the idea to make it known to the people around.

Ishmael Scott Reed a most notable twentieth-century African American writer was born at a place called Chattanooga, Tennessee on February 22nd 1938. Reed along with his family, at the age of four, moved to a place called Buffalo, in New York. These places become very lucky for Reed because in those places he was evidenced as a great and talented writer. Reed was born as a son of Henry Lenoir and Thelma Coleman. His interest in the newspaper reporting made him have a regular Jazz column in the *Empire State Weekly*, a local black newspaper further he got the opportunity at the early age of fourteen. Thelma Coleman his mother was never married to his natural father, Henry Lenoir, but she got married to an autoworker named Bennie Reed and gave Reed the Surname.

Reed graduated from Buffalo's East High School in the year 1956 then later he started to attend Millard Fillmore College, which is the night division of the University of Buffalo. During the time he supported himself in the work at Buffalo public library system. A short story named *Something Pure,* in which he satirically portrayed Christ's return, as an advertising man paved the way for Reed to enrol in the day classes. It brought him the praise of an English Professor. Until 1960, Reed attended the University of Buffalo and then he withdrew due to financial conditions and social pressures.

He moved into the notorious Talbert Mall project, the two years he spent there provided him, a painful but at the same time a valuable experience of dependency and urban poverty. During these last years in Buffalo he moderated a controversial radio program for thc station WVFO, he has also acted in several local stage productions. Reed prevails as the best known satirical novelist, and even as a most respectable essayist, editor and poet. His four collections of poetry namely, *Catechism of D Neoamerican HooDoo Church* in the year 1970, *Conjure* in the year 1972, *Chattanooga* in the year 1973 and *Secretary to the Spirit* in the year 1977 have identified him as a profound African American poet. Maryemma Graham discusses the view of Reginald Martin about Reed:

The issue of Reed's relationship to the black aesthetic is surely an intriguing one, but it is debatable whether Reed's work is principally a black aesthetic project, defined as specifically as Martin does. A more valuable set of clues to Reed would result from exploring his relationship to modernism and postmodernism, to folk realism and naturalism, and to those Afro-American writers who have embraced these traditions. (593)

Reeds writing have proved to be incredible and most of the writers after reading his works felt astonished that he has been into various themes and he has discussed those themes in a very frank manner, much of his novel discuss modernism and postmodernism. The issues he creates and detects in his fiction proves his mastery in handling the subject. The effort he has taken to discuss a specific issue from a completely new angle is appreciable. As mentioned by Maryemma Graham there is no doubt about the fact that the themes of Reed have been embraced by the other writers of his period.

Reed began to experiment with fictional works, after reading the works of the novelist Nathaniel West. During the year 1956, when he was at the University of Buffalo,

Reed showed his first short story, this story was about an alienated young Black man. One of Reed's professors got so much impressed with him and he arranged day classes for Reed in the University. It was in the year 1960 Reed got tired of his college and he dropped out of his college and joined his job at the *Empire State Weekly*. From then, two years later he moved to the city of New York at the age of Twenty Two.

When Reed was in Manhattan, he joined the black poetry collective which was innovative, it hold the name Umbra Workshop. At the Umbra Workshop he wrote visionary poems, he did it because he got influenced by the poets like William Blake and William Butler Yeats. After that, he started to construct the African American mythology, which has become his central work later. During that time period, he supported himself by writing for the weekly named *Newark Advance*, which was in New Jersey, during the year 1965. He developed into an editor for the paper and in the same year, he co-founded one of the original underground newspapers *East-Village Other* along with Walter Bowart.

Adaptation has become paramount in various circumstances furthermore in general adaptation increases the chance or quality of surviving in a particular environment. Adaptation has been connected with an evolutionary process that would enable various human beings to better live in their particular surrounding. The adaptive response has been associated with adaptation along with, human beings face a succession of challenges in the environment in which humans live during the process of progress. People show flexibility to the imposed conditions according to their mindset. The process of behaving in a flexible manner improves the resilience of people to varying environments.

Philosophers and even natural historians from ancient times accept adaptation as an observable fact of life. Based on their liberated views on evolution, the perception or the explanation of adaptation differed. Adaptation determines the final cause of every attempt that human beings take. Adaptation does not have a physical form and it has not been a part of the physical body. It has been connected with psychology further adaptation has been a primary process that acts based on the human psychic part. Adaptation does not end up with visual traits, inhuman the process of adaptation has been quite complex.

Based on the behavioural aspects of an individual, the person gets adapted to or not to the environment in which he or she is in. The concept of adaptation involves adjustment and getting adjusted to the new conditions. The adaptive capacity of every individual varies according to their own psychological aspects. H.G Wells in his science fiction *The Time Machine* explained the process of adaptation that:

It is a law of nature we overlook, that intellectual versatility is the compensation for change, danger, and trouble. An animal perfectly in harmony with its environment is a perfect mechanism. Nature never appeals to intelligence until habit and instinct are useless. There is no intelligence where there is no change and no need of change. Only those animals partake of intelligence that have to meet a huge variety of needs and dangers. (73)

The idea of adaptation provides perseverance to the particular person to understand the interaction with other humans and to interpret things with intensity. Adapting to the atmosphere supports people to face the challenges and opportunities of the atmosphere in an optimistic way.

Life was not easy even for our ancestors furthermore the ancestors also faced the problems like injury, disease and death. It was only through the magical word adaptation the ancestors also survived in the world of challenges and the ancestors have even passed their strength to their forthcoming generations to face the problems.

The African Americans also adapt to various environments to survive, most of the African Americans sing during their work time, African Americans had the habit of telling stories to their children. Most of them spend much of their time in music, the other people who do not indulge themselves in such activities, after looking at them, started to adapt the technique to release their stress and thus started their own adaptive technique. Later, these adaptive techniques framed their culture. Since the people get into trouble most of the time, their faith in God increased and the songs the people sing were oriented with Gods and it increased their faith in God and hope.

Since the late 1960s, Reed spent much of his time on the West Coast. Reed became disenchanted with the East Coast literary establishment and then he settled in Oakland, California. There he entered the job of lecturing at the University of California at Berkeley. Reed noted the election of Ronald Reagan to the presidency. It was a turning point that marked a new era for the Americans, who demand all of their excessive whims, it happened during the year 1980. After that Reed wrote about that in his book *The Terrible Twos* in the year 1982, he used the characters the legend Santa Claus and his assistant Black Peter.

In this book, he has illustrated the state of affairs as the one which particularly threatens the black people. Reed has used a contemporary setting to attack the exploitative nature and Reagan administration of the American economic system. This novel portrays President Dean Clift as a mindless figurehead, manipulated by an oil cartel, that has supplanted the real Santa Claus. Nance Saturday, Reed's African American detective, sets out to discover St. Nicholas's place of exile. According to the title of the novel, the United States acts as selfishly and irrationally as the proverbial two-year-old. The main theme of the novel was about the manner in which a few avaricious people seek vast wealth at the expense of the majority of Americans.

In the novel *The Terrible Twos*, Reed has expressed about Christmas during the year 1980 and the people suffered a lot during that particular Christmas. Reed has declared that the people behaved in a very selfish manner and the President was not caring about his duty. The men around him were planning to destroy the surplus people in the country. The plan framed by the men around the President was named 'Operation Two Birds'. People faced issues and the characters in all sectors of society had their own problems to be solved. People were trying to get adapted to their environment to make their wishes come true.

The people belonging to all the sectors faced many issues, the weather was freezing, the common people struggled a lot to bear the weather. The rich people were not disturbed by the freezing cold weather, the rich people had a very good Christmas and the people enjoyed rich gifts. Common people were not able to adapt to that condition due to political issues and also because of the weather. The economical fluctuation has created a great impact on the people who struggle to run their daily life. The wealthy people were having a great Christmas in spite of the inflation and the worst climatic condition.

Reed has disclosed regarding the condition of wealthy people who do not feel any disturbance that "They are comfortable, well-off even. Regardless of how high inflation remains, the wealthy will have any kind of Christmas they desire, a spokesman for Neiman- Marcus announces. Their gifts range from $100 gold toothpicks to $30,000 Rolls Royces" (TWOS 5). Reed has further discussed two bosses Herman and George who were discussing their business.

After the discussion about the business George has inquired about Herman's son, Herman has stated that his son has gone to the seminary and he faces many disputes. Herman has stated that all the members in the seminary face strict orthodox rules and further his son's position in the seminary has created a lot of disputes. Reed has specified that people find it difficult to prove their identity not only in business but also in the service the people do. Reed has revealed about the condition of Herman's son who has been in the seminary that:

He said he was having some kind of dispute with his superiors. He said they
were too devoted to orthodoxy and ritual. He claims that he's a part of a new church. A church devoted to social and political issues. His position was the source of his troubles (TWOS 10-11).

Reed has discussed Vixen, who struggle a lot to live in the place and she faced issues in the workplace and also in her personal life. She longed to be with her husband Sam, but her husband concentrated on painting. Vixen always felt a kind of gap between her husband and herself. Reed has explained that "She [Vixen] wished she and her husband, Sam, were a family. They were drifting apart. During the holidays, she began to yearn for the old values.

Of home and hearth. Maybe it was her New England background" (TWOS 14). She was habituated with the life of old values and the life in which she live did not provide her comfort. She faced issues and she was not able to be comfortable with her husband from whom she never got love and care.

Reed has presented about Bob Krantz who was talking through the phone to his boss Mr Whyte. Both were discussing the arrangements for the inauguration, the arrangements were done with the heavy fund. Mr Whyte informed Krantz that he needs the white substance and Krantz promised to provide him with the same. Reed has described that "That white dustlike substance. You [Krantz] remember how when some were spilled on the rug everybody got down on all fours and sniffed the rug. It was so pleasant. You referred to it as snow, I [Mr. Whyte] believe" (TWOS 19). Reed has given the account of people who have got habituated to the practice of drugs.

Reed has defined the character Nance, who quit his law school because he felt that there has been no law in the country. Nance has been in the top position in the law school and when he dropped out it was a shock for his friends. Later, when a friend met Nance he asked for a reason and Nance explained that law was of no use since class and power has been dominant in the society.

Reed has presented about the people who quit from the place in which the people are interested in, due to the reason that the people could not agree with the condition which prevailed in the country. Nance was not able to accept the condition of the country, he reached the perception that even if he complete law it would not be useful and he has decided to quit law school. "We live out in Staten Island now. I have a law office down in the Village.

You know, Nance, never did understand why you didn't finish law school. You were at the top of the class. Why did you drop out? There's no law in this country. Only power and class—" (TWOS 26-27).

Oswald Zumwalt prepared many dishes, Jane his wife reached home when he was busy cooking, she helped herself with grape juice. Jane questioned that if someone would be joining them for dinner. Oswald informed that it would be the boss. Reed has discussed the words of the character Oswald that "The boss, he [Oswald] said. You know, since his wife died he's been a lonely man. She made a face. I hope you don't mind" (TWOS 29). Oswald wished to invite his boss because the boss felt lonely after the death of his wife. Reed has specified about Jane who wished to spend time with her husband, felt disappointed that the boss of her husband would join them for dinner.

Jane hated everything around her, Jane and her husband Oswald has decided to move to Montana. Jane felt it hectic to spend time in the city where both live, according to Oswald it was a silly decision to quit the place and to leave Montana. Oswald was much interested in business, he opted to be in the city. Jane hated the lifestyle in the city with skyscrapers and limousines, she liked her life to be filled with nature which was not possible with the city life. Reed has expressed the feeling of Jane through her words. About the disgusting life in the city, Jane has explained that:

Well, I'm [Jane] not going to be a nine-to-five copy editor for the rest of my life. I'm tired of the East. It stinks here. All of the contradictions of the capitalistic system are in plain view. The pitiful vagrants and the limousines with their shades drawn, the fascist impersonal skyscrapers. Hideous glass boxes. I haven't seen a bird or a wild tree in so long I forget what they look like. (TWOS 31)

Reed has specified about Bob Krantz, when Bob was at a meeting with Admiral Mathews, Reverend Jones, Robert Reynolds and other eminent men, a man entered with a telephone rested on a pillow. The man who entered informed Krantz that, his wife is at the call. After picking the call Bob shouted at his wife first and then felt sorry because it has been three months before he went to his home. Bob's wife informed that their son has passed away in a car accident. Bob informed his wife that he has been busy with business and he further informed his wife that he would send flowers through the secretary.

After answering the call Krantz continued talking to the delegates. Bob informed the delegates that "I'm sorry, gentlemen, you know how these minor domestic matters sometimes intrude upon the business at hand. Seems my son was killed in a car accident" (TWOS 55). Reed has portrayed the character, Bob Krantz that, he has been into his business all the time and he was least bothered about his family life. He has got adapted to the mechanical life of dealing with business and politics and it made him a person without emotions. After answering the call from his wife without any kind of emotion he continued talking to the delegates for hours together. Nazareth has explained about the incidents of *The Terrible Twos* Christmas by Reed that:

Reed situates the body of his story in 1990 and tries to set things right through the fictional re-creation of one of the country's central myths, that of Santa Claus. One of the corporations has bought the exclusive rights to Santa Claus and is building a Santa rival to Disneyland in the North. The poor have therefore lost their last, mythic helper. (458)

Reed has illustrated Zumwalt who got the rights to provide Santaclaus to all the toy dealers from the North Pole Corporation for which he works. Zumwalt was busy for the whole day explaining his plans to the congressman. After the congressman left, he turned to Santaclaus and shouted at him. Zumwalt has noticed Santaclaus who spoke with a lady at the Macy's reception.

He questions Santaclaus that according to the agreement the Santa can tell only Ho-Ho-Ho. Santaclaus said sorry, Zumwalt warned Santaclaus that he would be sent out of his position. Reed has defined about Zumwalt's words to Santaclaus that "O, don't play coy with me. I heard about it. At the Macy's reception downstairs. You were seen talking to a young lady. A buyer. You've forgotten that the contract requires you only to say Ho-Ho-Ho" (TWOS 67).

The Terrible Twos Christmas was very strange because of Santa's speech, Santa gave an inspirational speech and he made people understand the condition. He advised people to stop buying war toys and video games which add up to the turnover of the people in the high designation and the people in a high position make money out of the toys. Santa said that the people must make the businessmen understand their mistakes.

The people who listened to the speech of the Santa adapted to the advice given by the Santa and stopped buying toys, even the children followed the words of Santa. Martin has stated about the plan of White businessmen that "White businessmen have called a meeting to discuss the danger to their Santa Claus Plan. Big Business decides that they could corner the Christmas market if there were just one *official* Santa Claus" (46-47). All the plan of White businessmen was ruined by the effective speech of Santa.

Reed has provided the powerful words of Santa that "I [Santa Claus] say it's time to pull these naughty people off their high chairs and get them to clean up their own shit. Let's hit them where it hurts, ladies and gentlemen. In their pockets. Let's stop buying their war toys, their teddy bears, their dolls, tractors, wagons, their video games, their trees" (TWOS 97). Reed has manifested about the Christmas of *The Terrible Twos* in which all the people including the kids were able to turn their minds to the effective speech of Santa Claus.

Reed has described two men discussing their wife and kids changed their minds as not to buy anything for Christmas. Reed has explained about the men discussing their family that "It's OK with me. My kid said this morning that he didn't want anything for Christmas. The wife too. They heard Santa's speech and agreed with him" (TWOS 117). The people started to understand and to adapt to the situation of their place, everyone made up their mind to stand with Santa's words to fight against the prevailing cruelty.

In *The Terrible Twos* Reed has projected about the people in the highest position of the society would always try to enjoy and to earn profit. The people in the white house do not bother about the common people in the society. The common people were let to struggle in the freezing worst weather. The people in the society work very hard to adapt to the changing world and inflation. The people felt that everything happened due to the business in which the people who belong to the highest designation in the society like to have the overall welfare. The people at certain point change their minds to prove their positive identity by making their minds adapt to their surroundings.

In *The Terrible Twos*, Reed has revealed the issues that happen in the white house. The weather was very cold and the people who could not adapt to the weather condition died. The weather did not affect the people in the higher designation in the country moreover the higher officials enjoyed Christmas with joy. President Dean Clift after the electrocution of his wife and the visit of Saint Nicholas has changed a lot. Black Peter who got habituated to his ventriloquist techniques planned with body-snatching to make the people aware of the happenings around them.

Reed has presented about the visit of Saint Nicholas has changed the life of many people, President was sent to the sanatorium after the interview in which he stated that he met Saint Nicholas. People met Nicholas when the time was hard and when the people struggled to adapt to the environment. Saint Nicholas met many people and made them understand the originality and the truth. Thus Nicholas helped the people to attain their social identification. The people behaved in a selfish way blindly following their principles in the groups. The visit of Saint Nicholas helped them to achieve their social identification.

Reed wrote *The Terrible Threes* in 1989, which acts as a sequel to his novel *The Terrible Twos*. The novel *The Terrible Threes* talks about the political condition of the city and the fraudulence happening around it. In this novel, several things happen at once. The action prevails rapid and simultaneous moreover the novel has explained the idea that people of the society are haunted by past crimes. Reed has drawn the characters Santa Claus and Black Peter, sometimes known as a Black helper. Both the character played a major role in both *The Terrible Twos* and in *The Terrible Threes*. The novel bared Reed's distinctive message, a threat, a promise, a prediction and the awful truth about the land of free and the home of brave.

In *The Terrible Threes* Reed has projected about the Christmas which happened after four years from *The Terrible Twos* Christmas. Reed has provided connectivity with the two novels. The characters in the novel have been receiving help through the saintly figures Black Peter and Saint Nicholas. The characters that could not get adapted to the environment, after getting visited by the saintly figures, felt fresh and decided to lead a new life. The saintly figures helped the common people a lot to make them get adapted to the emerging issues and to tackle the issues in a very eminent way.

Reed has noted about the habituation of people at higher places, the people at the higher designation would always have someone to take their fault if caught. Jesse Hatch met Reverend Jones to discuss the letter written by the late Admiral Mathews. Hatch was much scared that if anything gets revealed then the group would be sent to jail. Reverend explained that there would be someone always to take their fault. Reverend has stated that if congress rises against them then the group would offer them a good deal. Reed has conveyed the words of Reverend that "Don't worry, Jesse, it'll blow over. We have someone to take the fall. If Congress acts up we'll throw them a piece of meat. Kosher meat" (THREES 9).

Reed has concentrated on the characters Reverend and his wife, Reed has stated that "The paintings filled the three bedrooms of the upstairs, the garages and the basements. Sometimes she [Reverend's wife] would paint for three days, and go without food. It kept her busy, and the Reverend figured that it was good therapy" (THREES 15). Jones followed a very simple life, he rarely visited his wife. His wife spent much of her time painting. She painted the same pictures again and again. Her paintings were hung all over their house in the bedroom and in the garage. She was taken care of by a caretaker. The Reverend thought that the painting can serve as a good therapy for her.

Nance has adapted to many situations, he quit law school and his marriage life was not the best for him. Nance did the detective work for Joe baby during *The Terrible Twos* Christmas. For Nance's good work, Joe baby has given him a good amount of money, Nance has been working as a driver from the time he received money from Joe Baby as a gift. Reed has narrated that "A man opened the door of the black limousine that Joe Baby had given him and got in. "I hope you're not in a hurry," Nance said" (THREES 24). Nance got habituated as a driver and he has been serving people as a driver.

Reed has focused on the adapted condition of the president Dean Clift, the President did not care for anything. He was not frightened at the men at the white house, he was ready to set things right. After the electrocution of his wife and after the visit of Saint Nicholas, he has changed a lot. The President was very sad after the death of his wife moreover Nicholas appeared and showed the truth in the eyes of the President. After the incident President has made up his mind to narrow down things.

Reed has identified about the adaptation of president through president's words that "Dean walked to the window, and stared through the bars which were misshapen by the snow. I was just along for the ride. I didn't care about what Reverend Jones was up to. But after Elizabeth, and Nicholas, after those experiences, I changed. If I ever get out of here, I'm going to straighten things out" (THREES 46).

Jack Frost the man, who worked for Oswald Zumwalt, has joined to work as a floor walker and troubleshooter for Elder Marse after *The Terrible Twos* scandal. Marse and Jack discussed the business and the demand for the toy of

Black Peter has been shooting up. Marse has stated that cvcn during thc football match intcrval thc pcoplc startcd to shout Black Peter's name. Marse allotted work for Jack to bring Black Peter to pump up their business and sales. Reed has analyzed the businessmen who get updated to the current trends and would like to get adapted completely. Reed has provided the words of Elder Marse about the character, Black Peter that:

> This Black Peter is bigger than Michael Jackson. Why, during the intermission of football games, crowds are shouting Black Peter, Jack. I think this Black Peter is just the thing that we need to put into the cash register. And just think, it was only a few years ago that the public was screaming for his skin, after that playboy Boy Bishop, that hippie, revealed how Black Peter took over his group and forced him out. (THREES 55)

Reed has also defined the adaptation that happened in the life of the imposter, Black Peter. From the above lines, Reed has narrated that, during one situation people were in complete rage on the imposter Black Peter because he took over the group of Boy Bishop and tried to bring the place under his control. The time has changed, instead of hatred, the people started loving him. People admire Black peter and even shout his name in groups to show their love for him.

Reed has given an account of Black peter that he has been searched by most of the people around. Black Peter has been living in a cave underneath Manhattan, he send his followers to steal food for him since he got into the issue of *The Terrible Twos* Christmas. He has adapted to a new life, most of his followers went and joined in the other groups. In particular, the group members have joined in Reverend Jones Gospel group. Reed has examined the condition of

Black Peter that:

Most of the white dreds who'd followed him had returned to their suburbs, after polite, middle-class plea bargaining. Many had moved on to prep school or joined Reverend Jones's Christian majority, which was signing up students by droves on the campuses. The remaining ones had become fed up with the squalid life and were getting on another's nerves. (THREES 57)

Reed has disclosed the popularity of Black Peter, the news about the popularity he gained, reached him through Jack Frost. Black Peter got scared when he met Jack Frost at the entrance of the cave. Jack Frost made him understand his popularity moreover Black Peter was shocked and surprised after listening to Jack's words about his popularity. Black Peter thought about his complete transition, he was popular due to the Madison Square incident but later he possessed much familiarity and people loved him a lot. Reed has identified the popularity of Black Peter in the following words:

There were Black Peter dolls, Black Peter bicycles, Black Peter wine, Black Peter perfumes, Black Peter pennants, and even something called the Black Peter look. There was a rap group called the Black Peters. Black Peter was stunned. He had been the public's goat for four years, ever since the Madison Square Garden riots, and now he was on the rise again. Proving once again that the raw market values of capitalism were chaotic. (THREES 59)

Beechiko respected Mr Longsfellow and she came along with him to his house to offer service to him. Beechiko took all the care of Mr Longsfellow, she supervised the house cleaning done by Samantha and Teddy Crawford. Beechiko habituated living in the place of Mr Longsfellow, she worked on her second book during the evening times.

Reed has elucidated about Beechiko that she did her work and at the same time she concentrated on the complete care of Mr Longsfellow. Reed has revealed about the service of Beechiko for Mr Longsfellow that:

She [Beechiko] was happy serving Mr. Longsfellow and writing, in the evening, her second book about the treatment of Japanese women in the novels of Japanese men. Having indicted most of the Japanese male writers in history, she was completing her last chapter on sexism. Her first book was receiving good reviews. (THREES 88-89)

The Crawford's had a very hard time after the arrival of Beechiko at their place, she supervised each and every work the Crawford's did. Mr Longsfellow supported Beechiko a lot, Beechiko followed Crawford's work schedule. Crawfords felt it very difficult because the workers were not into such tough work before. Beechiko made them work in a very dedicated manner. She checked and found even the simple fault the Crawfords did and instructed them to correct it. She also took special care of Mr Longsfellow's food and clothes. The Crawfords could not adapt to the strict rules of Beechiko and tried somehow to get escaped. Reed has displayed about the strict checking and following of Beechiko on Crawfords that:

With Mr. Longsfellow's vote of confidence, Beechiko ruled the roost.She made the Crawfords' lives miserable, being constantly on their case, prying into their cleaning schedule, going after them for every particle of dust they overlooked, for every faint ring in the bathtub. She personally supervised Mr. Longsfellow's meals, and the laundering of his clothes. (THREES 91)

Nola Pyne supported the conversion Bill and due to that, she faced opposition from most of the common people. One particular night she was visited by Saint Nicholas and

Judge Tany's spirit. After their visit, she has changed a lot because both have made her understand the originality by explaining the truth to her. The next morning she woke up earlier, she put all the pills and drinks into the sink. Nola decided to get adapted to the truth and to get transformed. She prepared her own breakfast along she called the people in the court for a special session.

The chauffeur looked at her with surprise that, in all the five years she came down the stairs without any support. Reed has specified about the transformation in the character of Nola Pyne that "She [Nola Pyne] prepared her own breakfast and ate in the garden. She walked down the stairs and got into her limousine. Her chauffeur was shocked. This was the first time in five years that he didn't have to help her down the stairs, as she was recovering from a drunken stupor" (THREES 115).

In *The Terrible Threes* Reed has discussed the characters and the positive transformation in them. The characters change their mind after the visit of the saintly figures Black Peter and Saint Nicholas. Reed has revealed the characters who struggle a lot to get adapted, the characters made up their mind to get adapted to the situation after the visit of the saintly figures. Reed has shown that the characters fought a lot to prove their identity, Reed has also noticed the strange political condition in which the President does not have any hold. Even the president got adapted to the environment after the visit of Saint Nicholas.

In *The Terrible Threes*, Reed has expressed the connected plot of *The Terrible Twos* Christmas. In this novel, the characters of the fiction are visited by two saintly figures Black Peter and Saint Nicholas. The two saintly figures help people during their hard times to prove their social identification and show the truth in front of people to make them understand the good and evil that prevail in society. The people accept the words of the President that he has met Saint Nicholas.

Reed has explored the two saintly figures that compete with each other to prove their social identification as good spirits. The characters in the fiction habituate to the surroundings and do things based on the group to which the people belong. The people were guided to the right path by the visit of the saintly figures. Reed has shown the politics that rule the entire country and has proved even the President was in the hold of the group which plan to grab the goodness in a selfish manner.

Reed through his exploration of new concepts and unique detective techniques, has paved way for most of the readers to learn about various traditions and to develop their adaptive techniques to excel in life. Weixlmann has stated about Reed that "Not content to rest the case there, Reed proceeds actively to blend historical and fictional characters and accounts. Only when liberated from the arbitrary enclosures which society attempts to erect around the writer is he or she able to explore the full range of human thought and knowledge" (65).

Reed has a special place in African American literature and his works have proved to be very exclusive in the various aspects that have been the prime reason, those works impressed all sectors of people in the entire world. Reed's works convey the themes and ideas that are very new to the people and even the serious issues are discussed in a satirical and ironic aspect which projects the special talent that is hidden in Reed's work.

These unique characteristics help Reed to be on the top priority list of African American writers. His works stand as an epitome of African American culture and tradition.

Reed has also explored the distinct myths and their core concepts in his plot to provide an interesting link to his contemporary setup thus proving his in-depth knowledge of ancient histories. White has expressed his views on Reed's works, he has discussed that:

One of the leading satirists in contemporary black literature, Reed is best known for those novels in which he examines politics, religion, and technology as repressive forces. Although the central target of his work is Western civilization, Reed's primary concern in his writings is the establishment of an alternative black aesthetic. (355)

The main focus is on the inspection of the characters based on their behavioural aspects and analyzing the characters based on pliable techniques. The process of habituation has been well handled by Reed, the characters that change their mind to get adapted, step into a successful atmosphere whereas the characters that hesitate, end up with ruined fate. Reed has differentiated the character's embarrassment and prosperity as an after effect of the character's implementation of adaptive techniques since the process includes certain psychological motives.

REFERENCES

"Adaptation." *Debating Humanity: Towards a Philosophical Sociology*, by Daniel Chernilo, Cambridge UP, Cambridge, 2017, pp. 87–110.

Agarwal, Gyan C. "Human Cognition Is an Adaptive Process." *Behavioral and Brain Sciences*, vol. 14, no. 3, 1991, pp. 485–486., doi:10.1017/S0140525X00070813.

Anderson, John R. "Is Human Cognition Adaptive?" *Behavioral and Brain Sciences*,
vol. 14, no. 3, 1991, pp. 471–485., doi:10.1017/S0140525X00070801.

Bezner, Kevin, and Ishmael Reed. "An Interview with Ishmael Reed." *Mississippi Review*, vol. 20, no. 1/2, 1991, pp. 110–119.

Graham, Maryemma, and Jerry W. Ward, Jr, editors. "African American Literature From Its Origins To The Twentieth Century." *The Cambridge History of African American Literature*, Cambridge UP, Cambridge, 2011.

Martin, Reginald. "Ishmael Reed's Syncretic Use of Language: Bathos as Popular Discourse." *Modern Language Studies*, vol. 20, no. 2, 1990, pp. 3–9.

---. "New Ideas For Old: New Black Aesthetic." *CEA Critic*, vol. 50, no. 2/4, 1987,
pp. 90–104.

---. "The Free-Lance PallBearer Confronts the Terrible Threes: Ishmael Reed and the New Black Aesthetic Critics." *MELUS*, vol. 14, no. 2, Summer 1987, pp. 35–49.

Nazareth, Peter, and Ishmael Reed. "An Interview with Ishmael Reed." *The Iowa Review*, vol. 13, no. 2, 1982, pp. 117–131.

Nazareth, Peter. "Heading Them Off at the Pass: The Fiction of Ishmael Reed." *Review of Contemporary Fiction*, vol. 4, no. 2, Summer 1984, pp. 208–26.

Reed, Ishmael. *The Terrible Twos*. Dalkey Archive P, 1982.

---. *The Terrible Threes*. Dalkey Archive P, 1989.

White, Edmund. "Reed's Syncretic Words." *Contemporary Literary Criticism*, edited by Jean C. Stine and Daniel G. Marowski, vol. 32, Gale Research, 1985, pp. 355-56. Originally Published in *The Nation*, vol. 223, no .8, Sept. 1976, pp. 247-49.

Weixlmann, Joe, et al. "African American Deconstruction of the Novel in the Work of Ishmael Reed and Clarence Major." *MELUS*, vol. 17, no. 4, 1991, pp.

57–79.

Wells,H.G."TheTimeMachine." *Literature page,* 2003.

9 798885 307734

Printed by Libri Plureos GmbH in Hamburg, Germany